Copyright@somafolkart

All Rights Reserved.

All rights reserved. No part of these artworks can be reproduced or used in any form or by any means – including graphic, electronics or mechanical including photocopying, recording without the permission of the author.

The artworks of this book are intended for the personal and non-commercial use of the retail purchaser. They are not meant to be reproduced in form for commercial use.

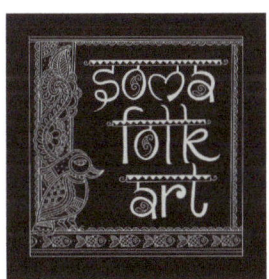

For any queries or feedback please visit

    Somafolkart

    Somafolkart

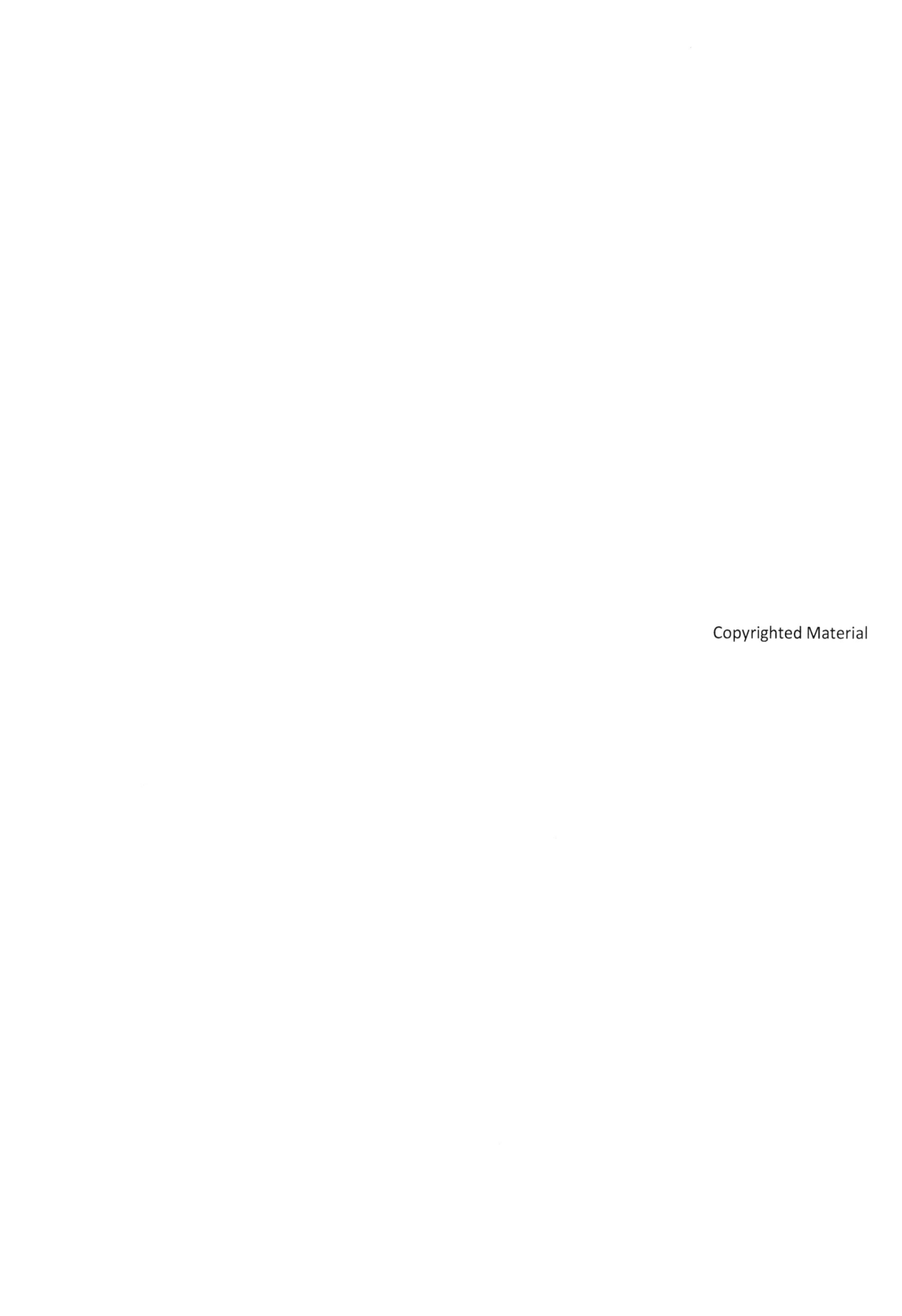

HER WORLD

Colouring Book Inspired by
Indian Folk Art

Dear Artists,

Thank you for purchasing "Her World". Hope you enjoy it as much I enjoyed creating it. If you like the artworks and enjoy bringing those to life with your own vibrant colours and designs, please spare few moments to give a review on Amazon. I would highly appreciate your honest feedback.

Yours sincerely,
Soma Chakraborty Debnath

Copyright@Somafolkart
All Rights Reserved

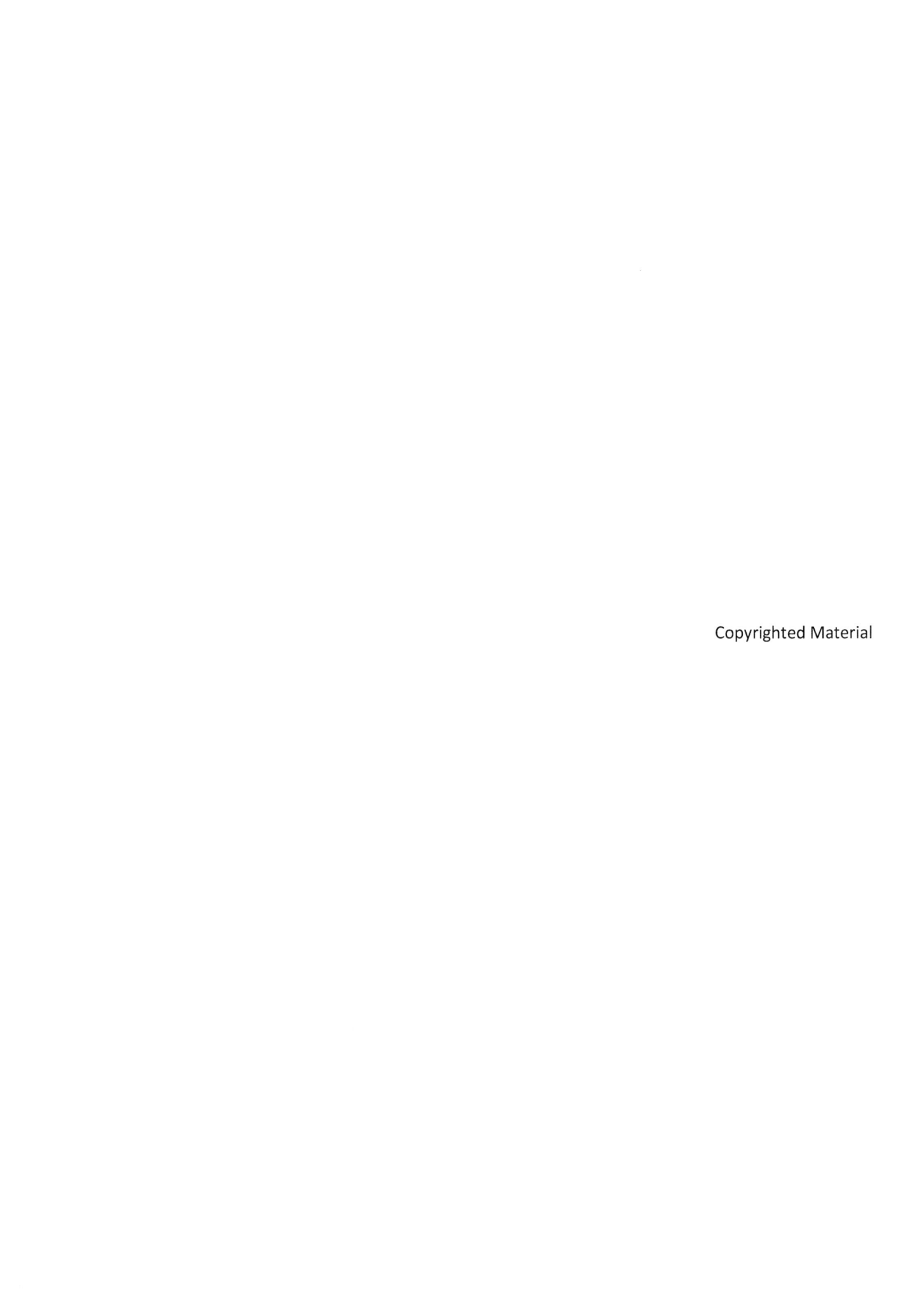

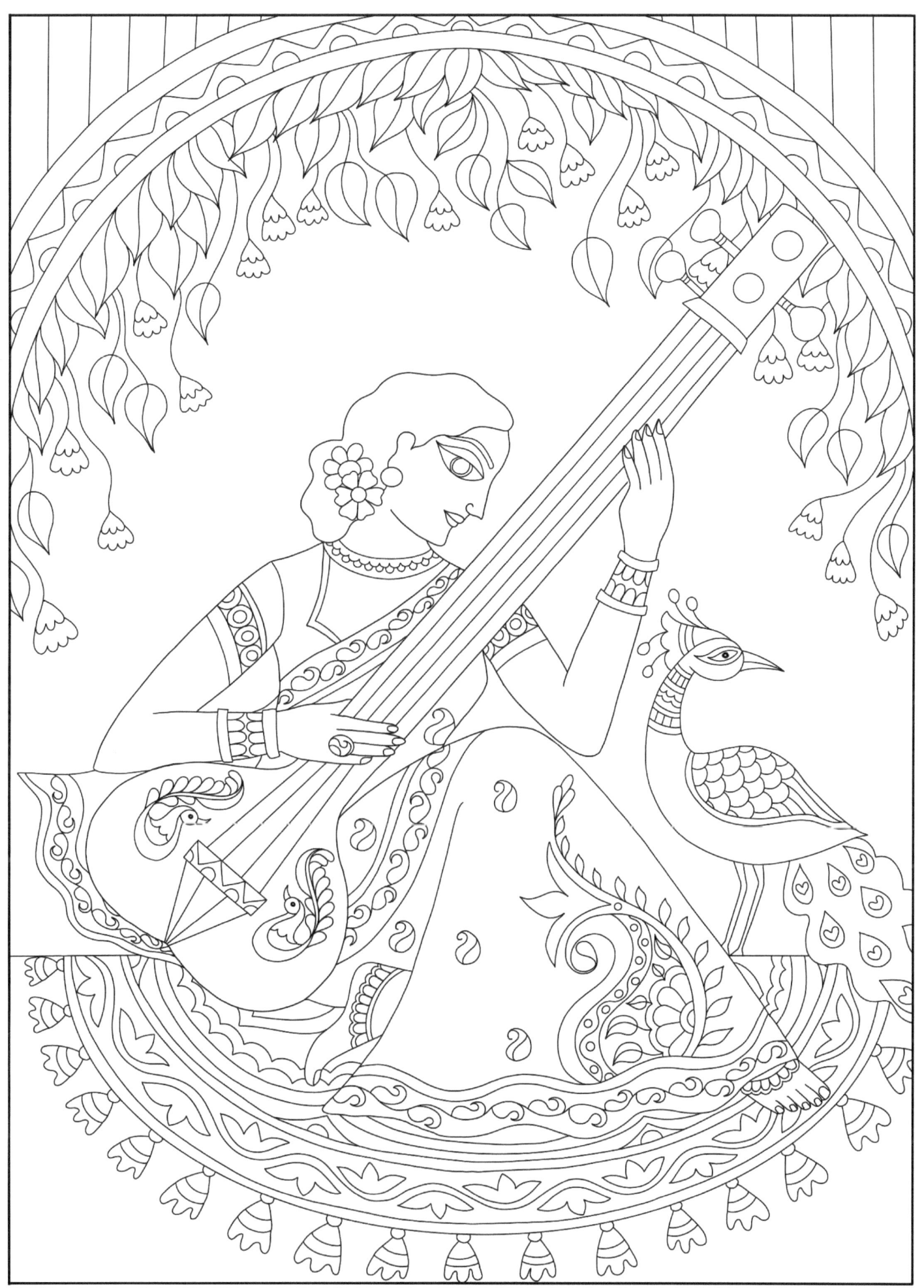

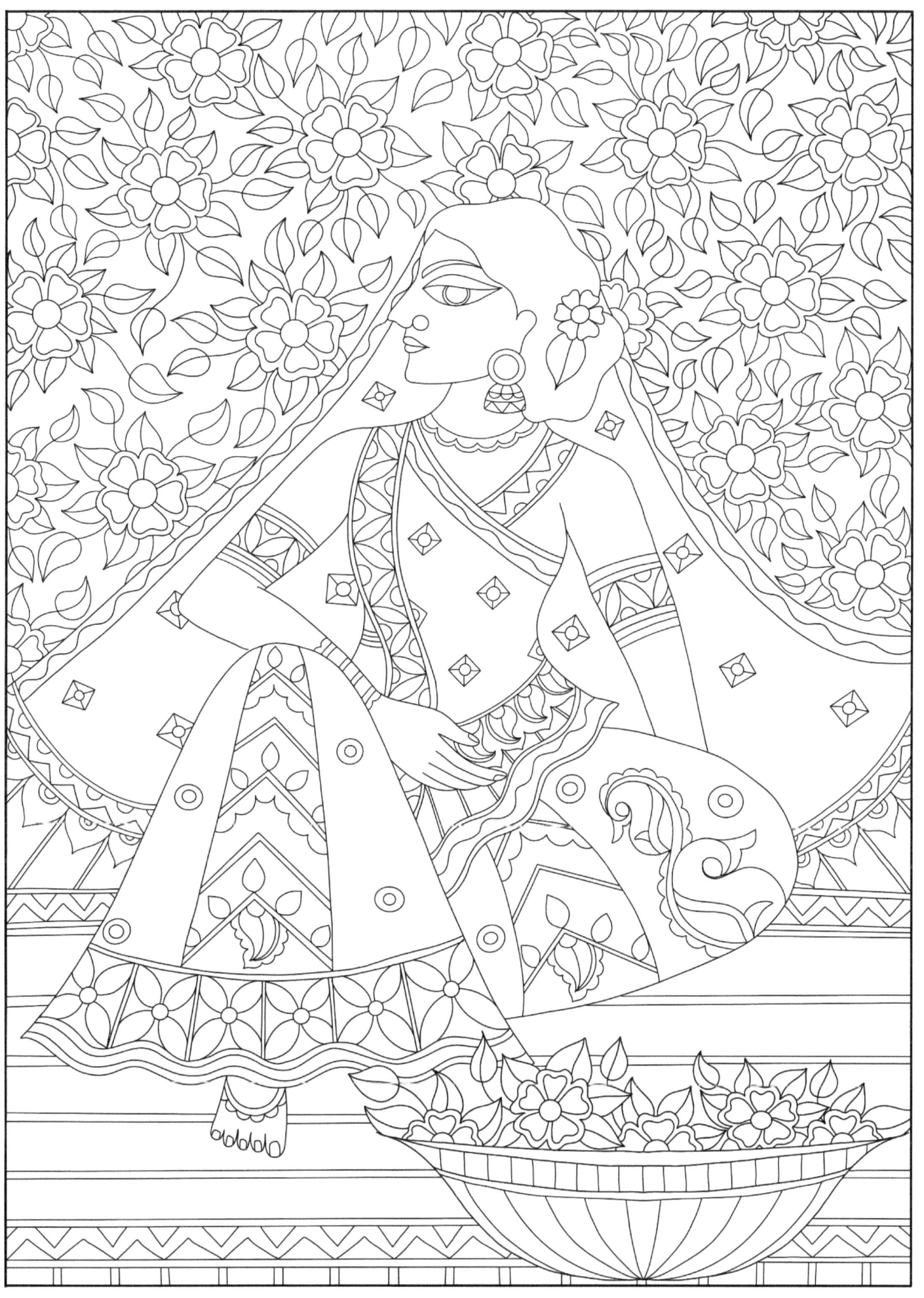

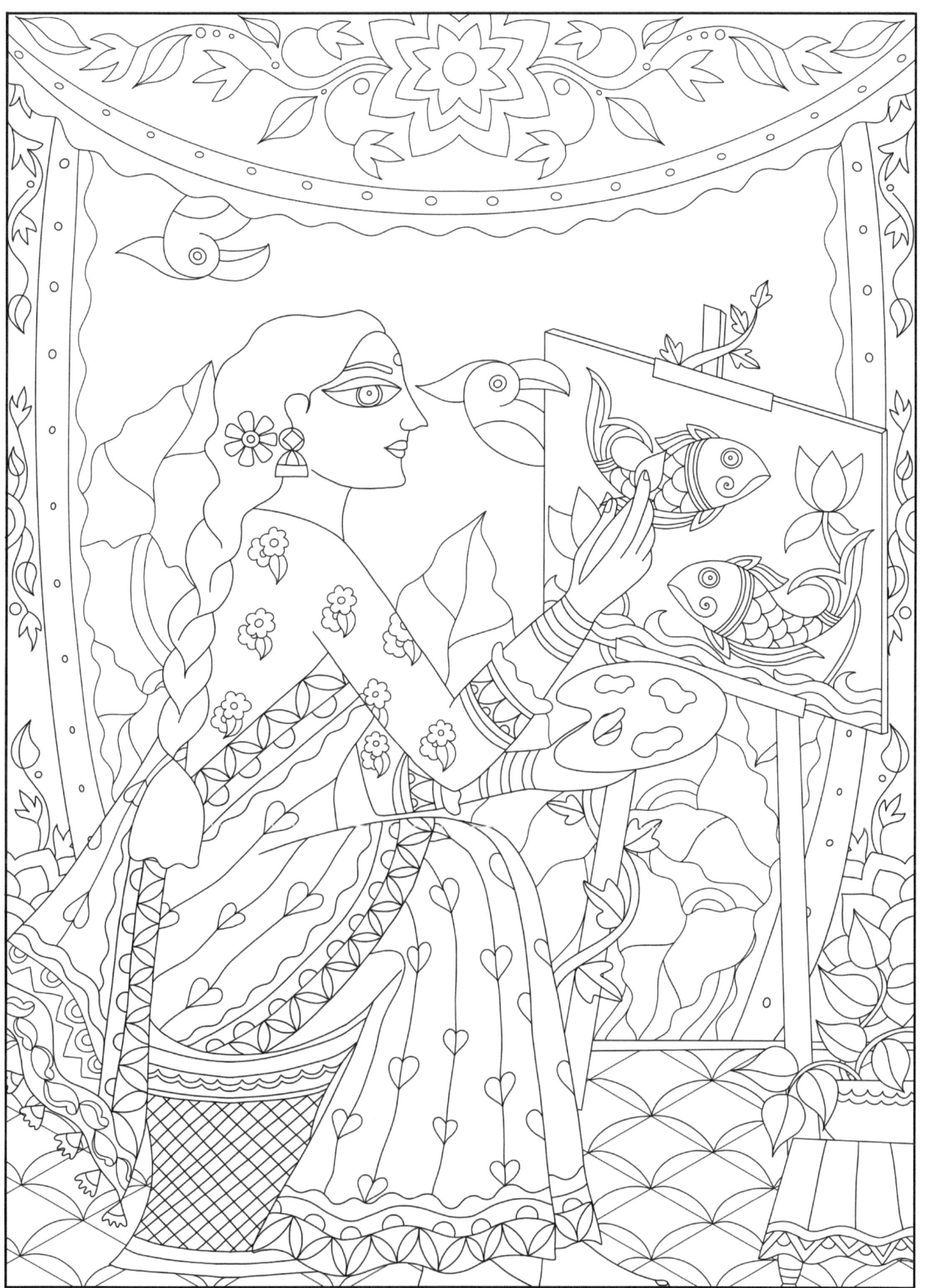

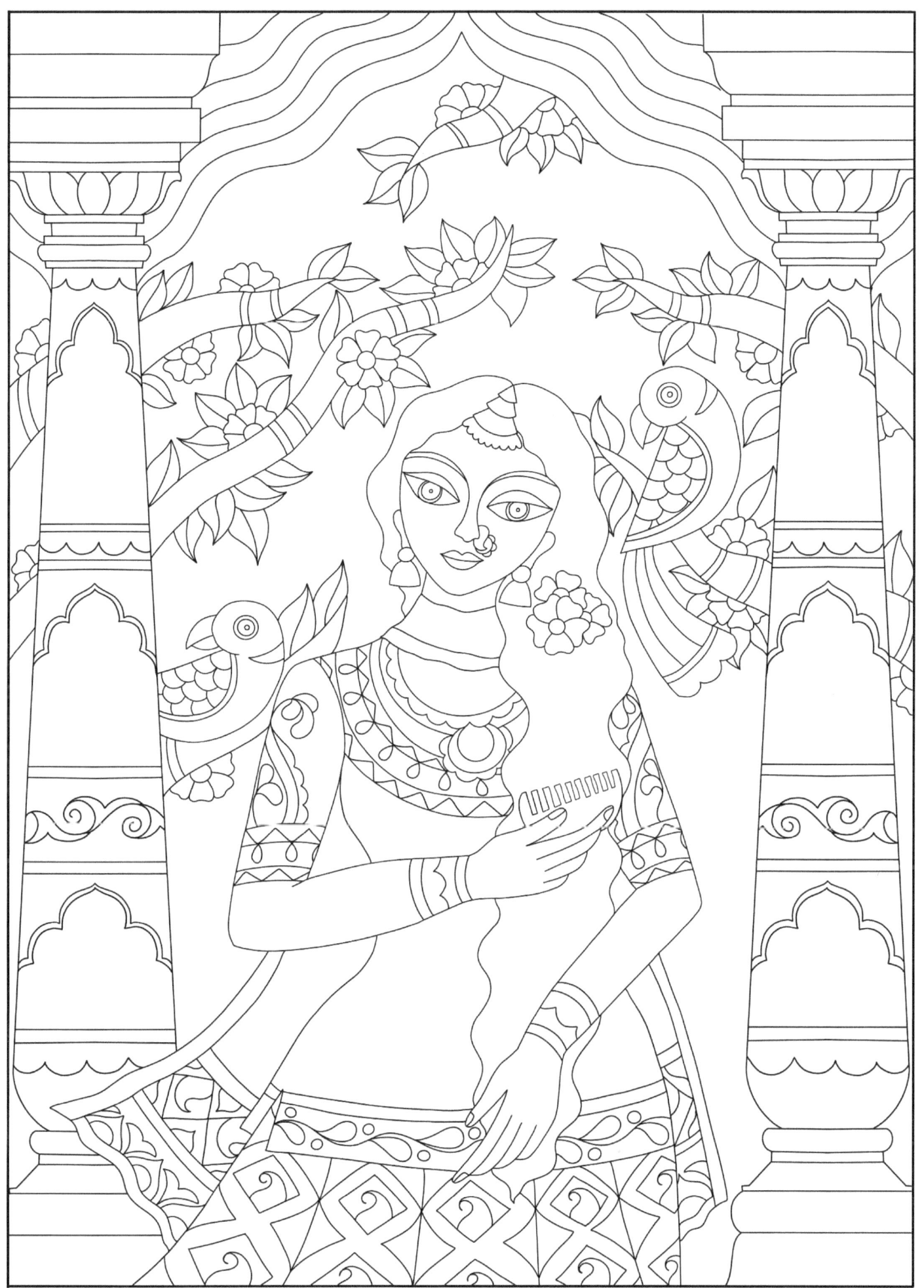

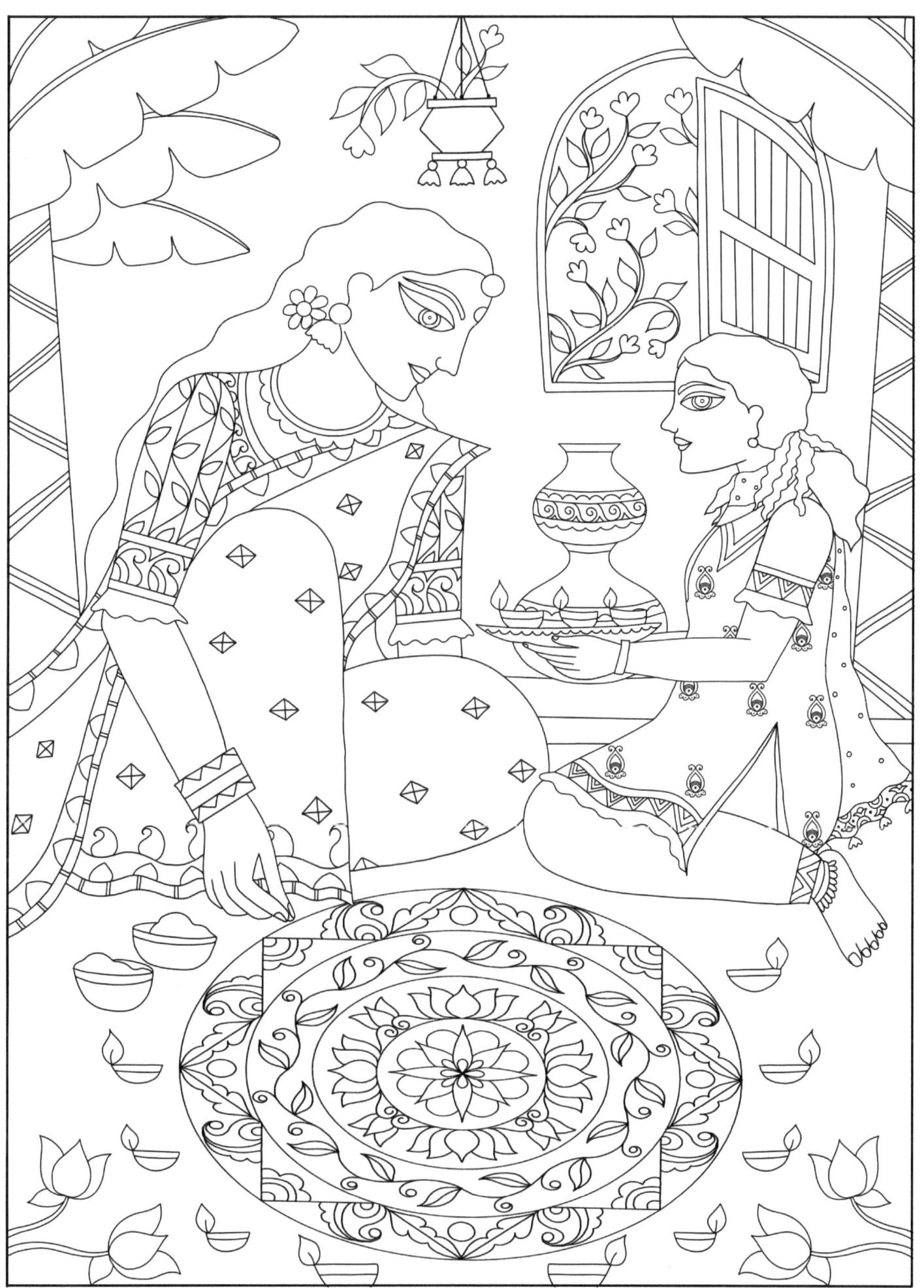

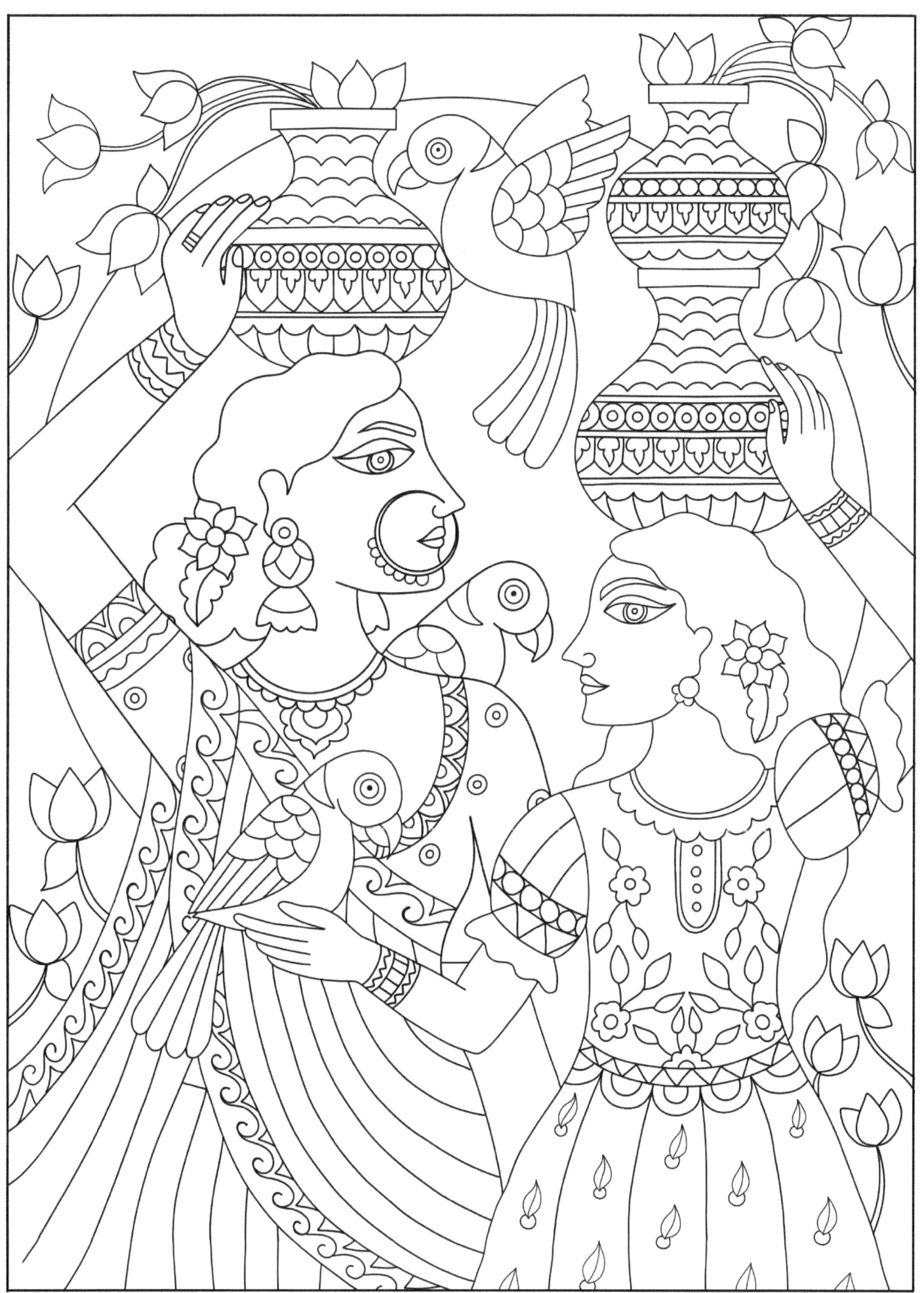

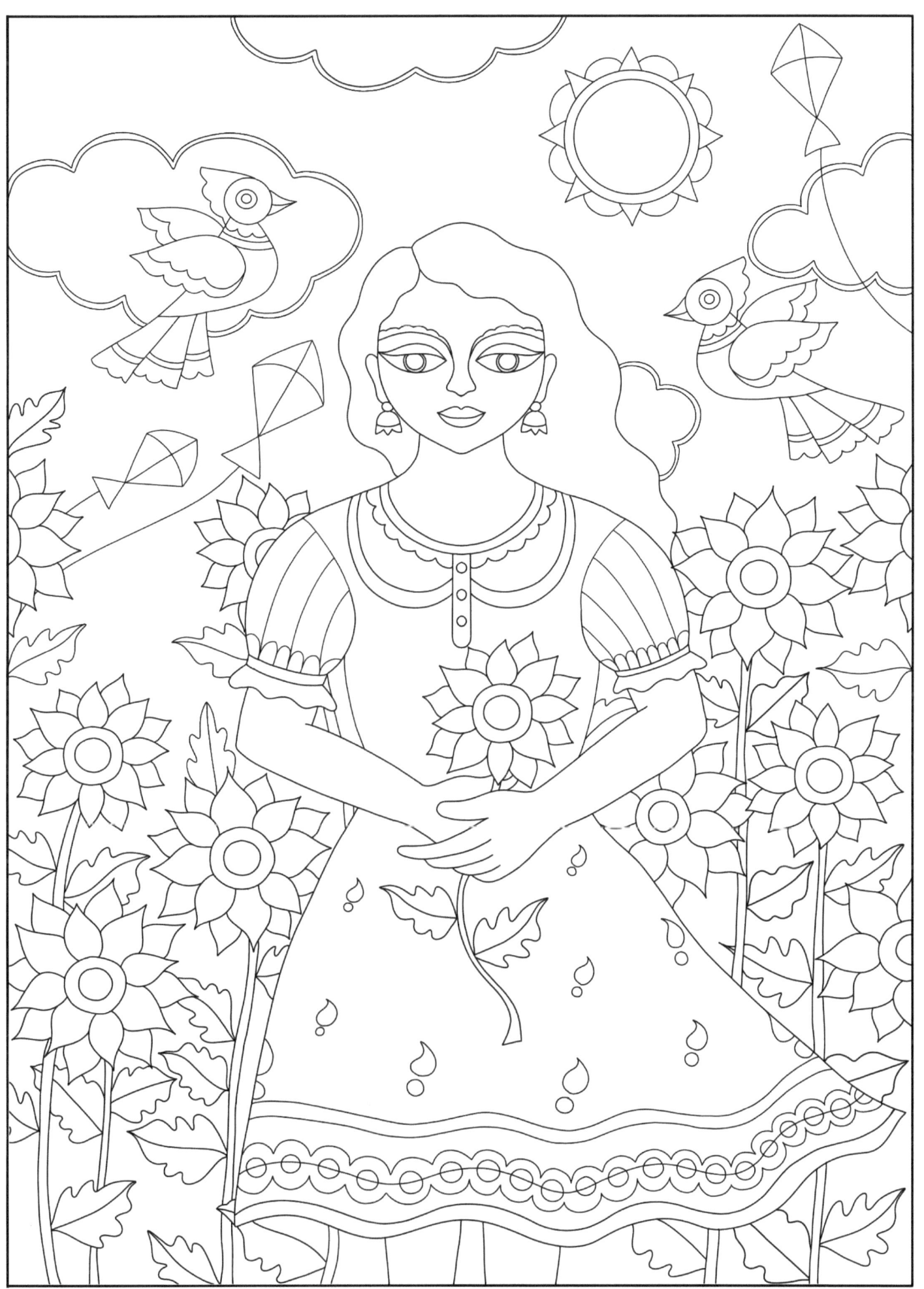

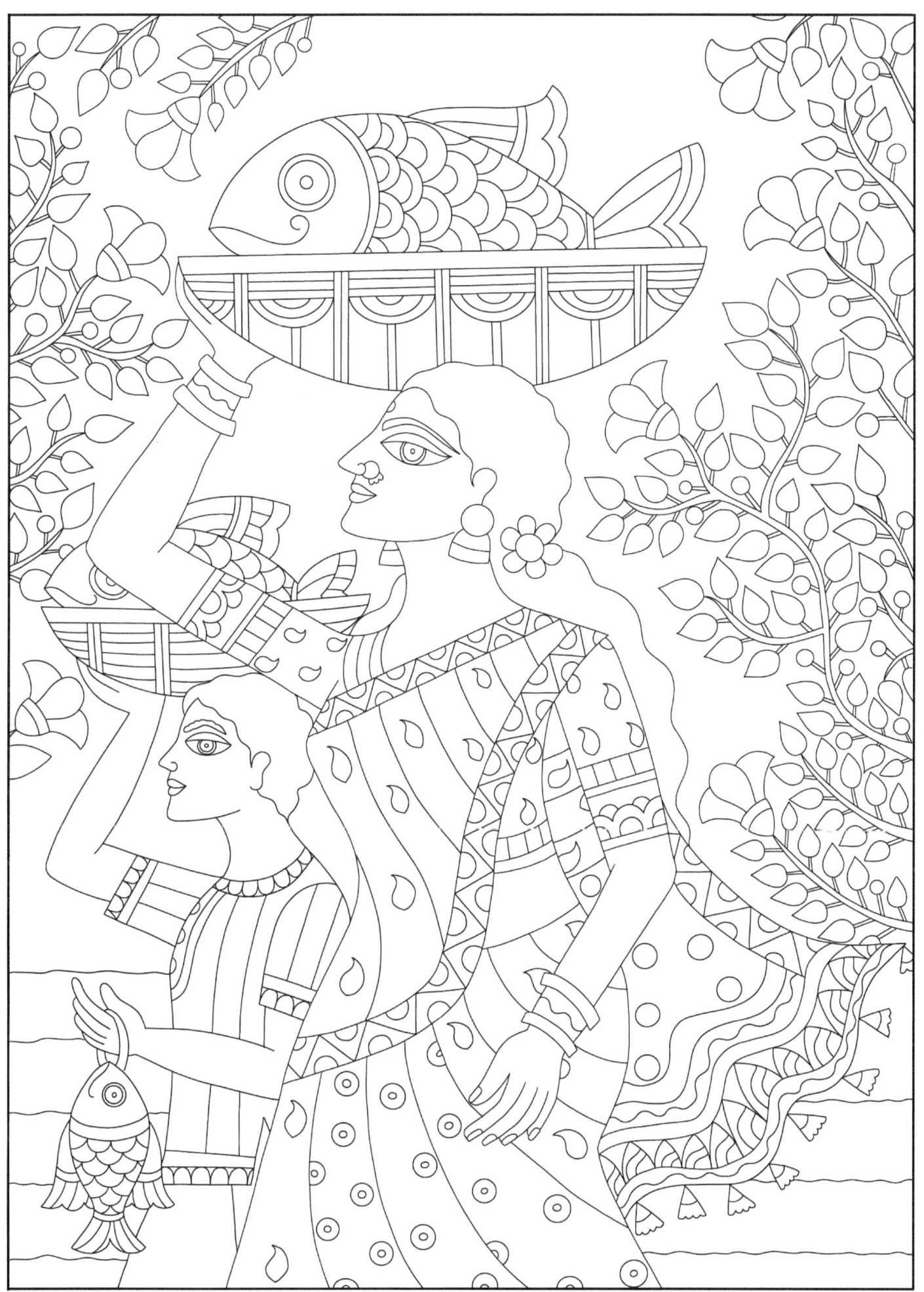

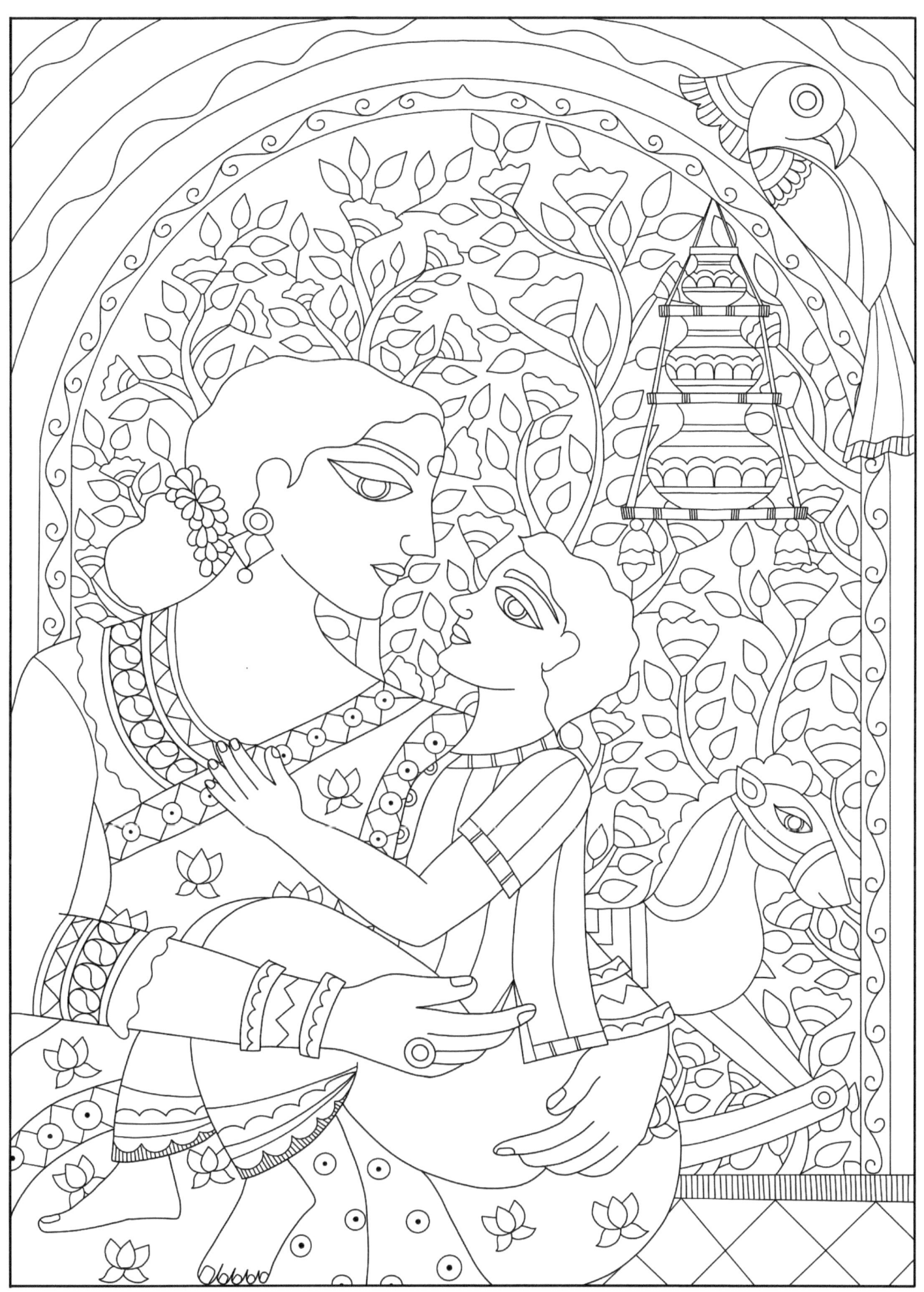

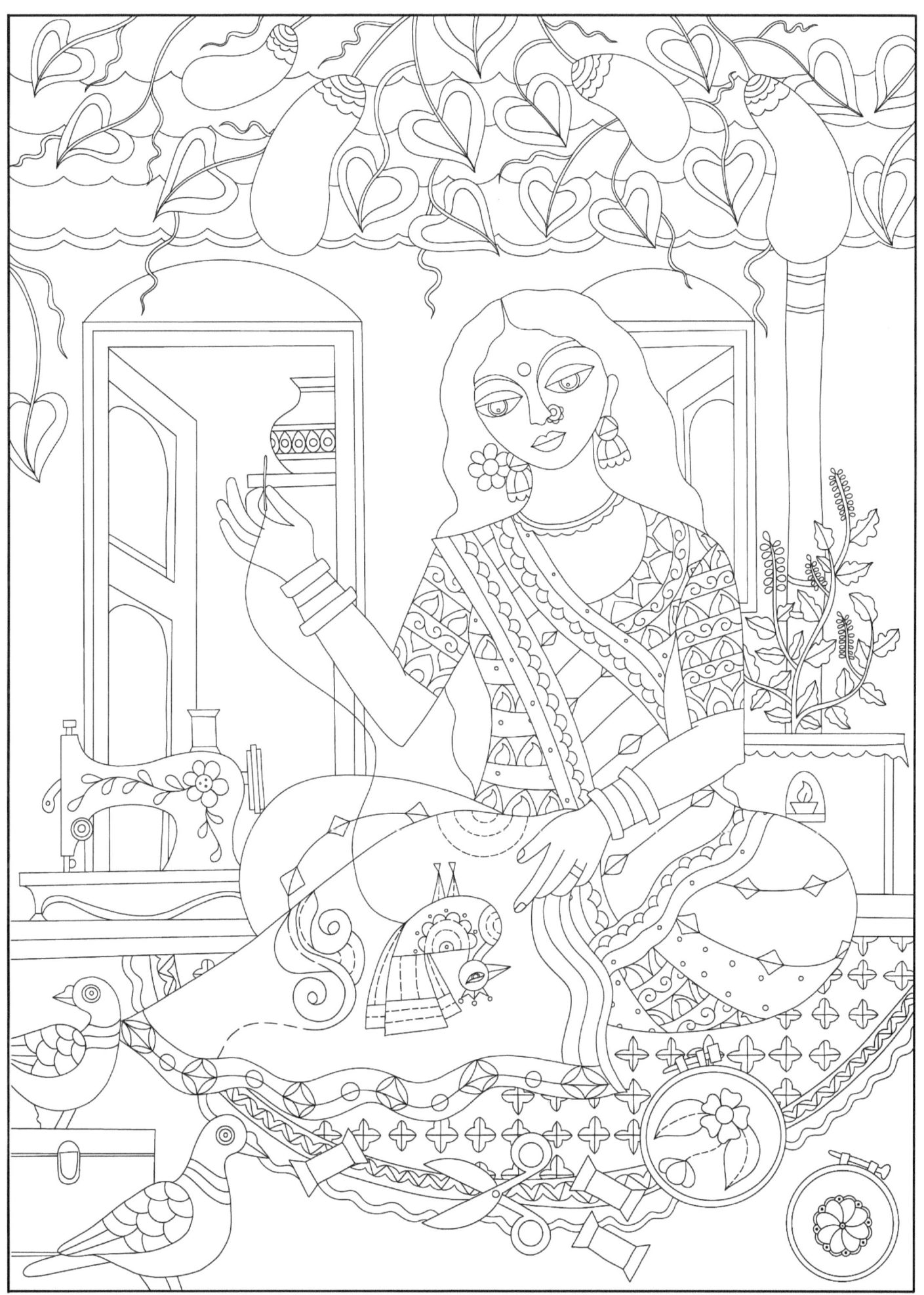

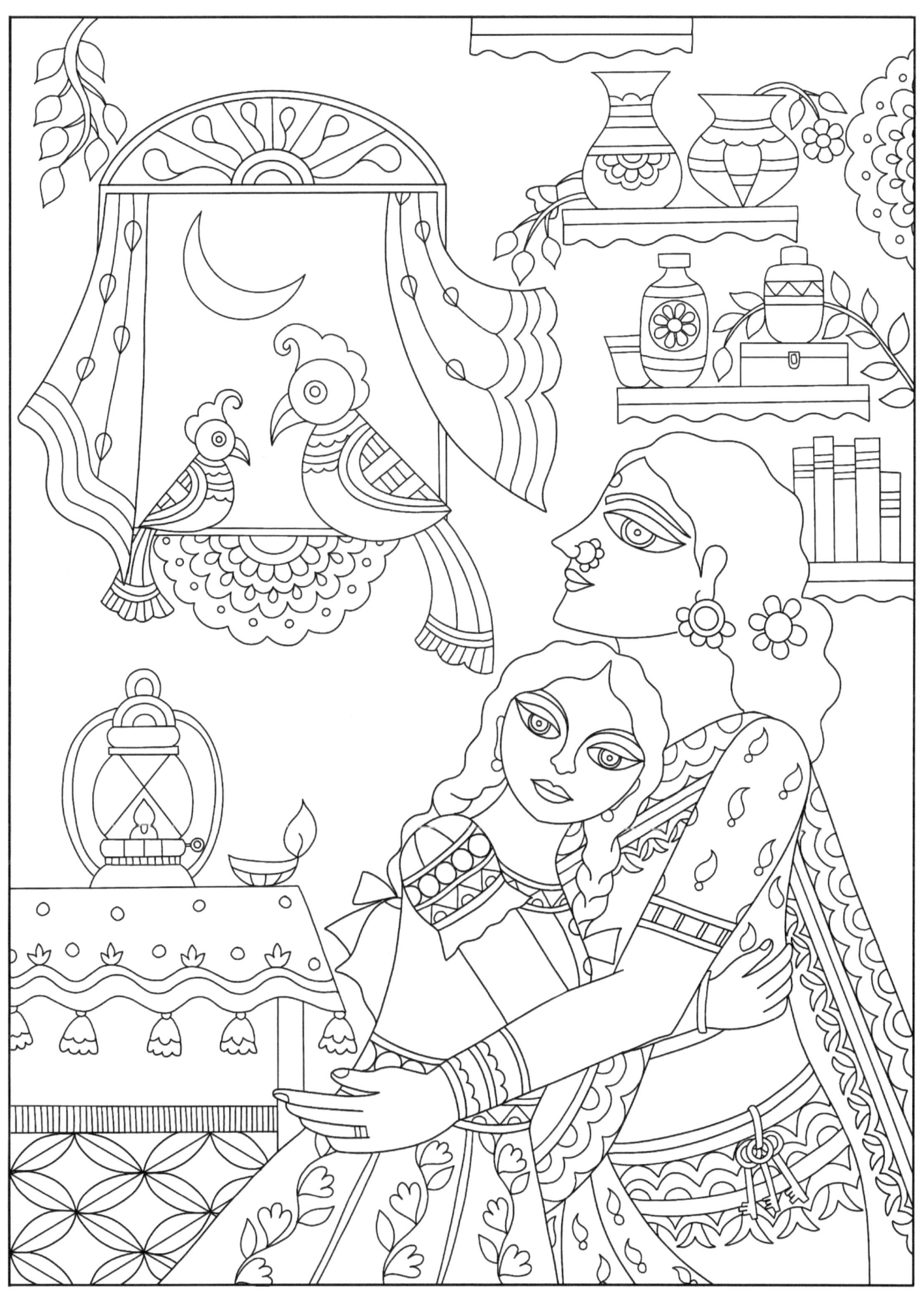

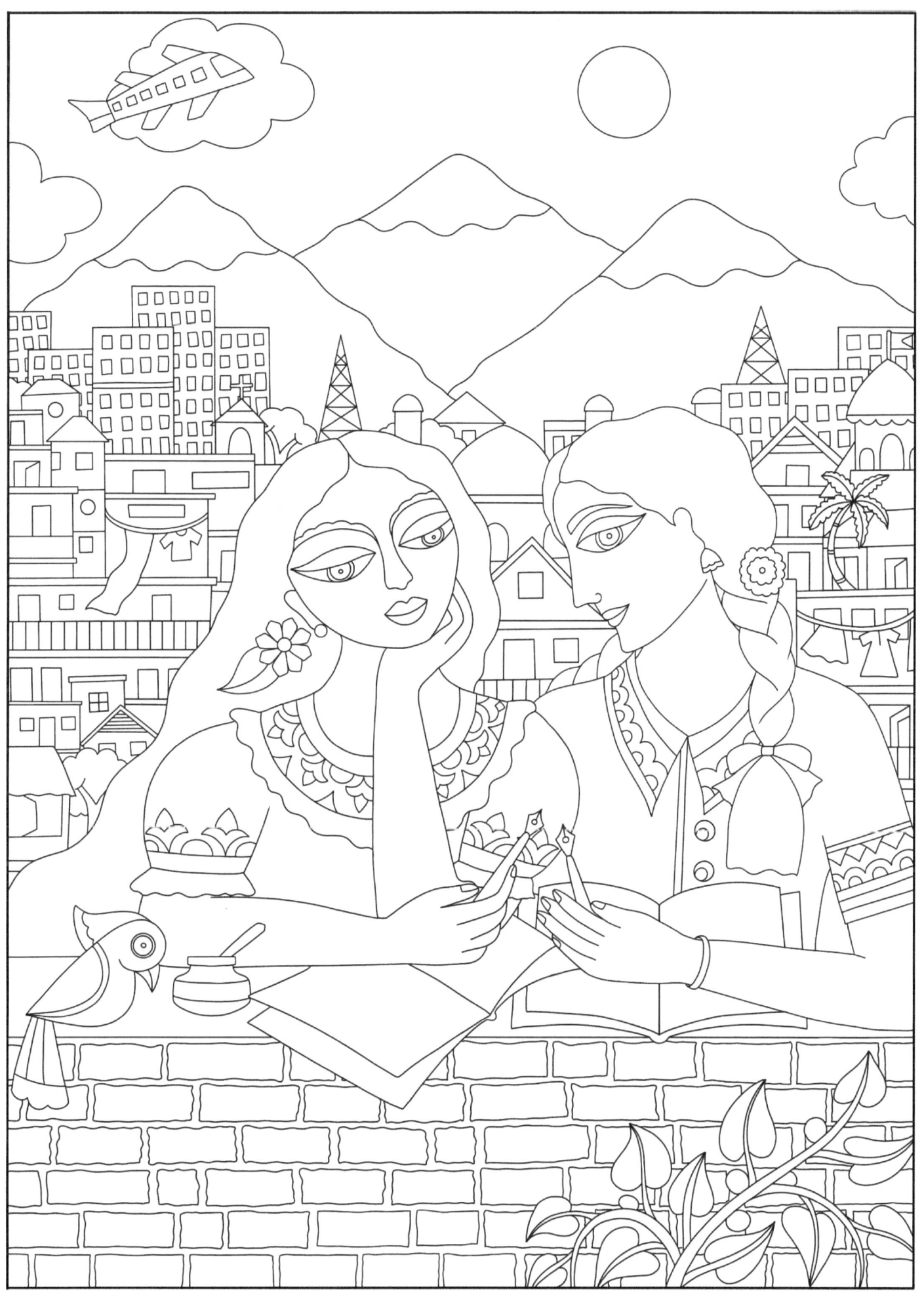

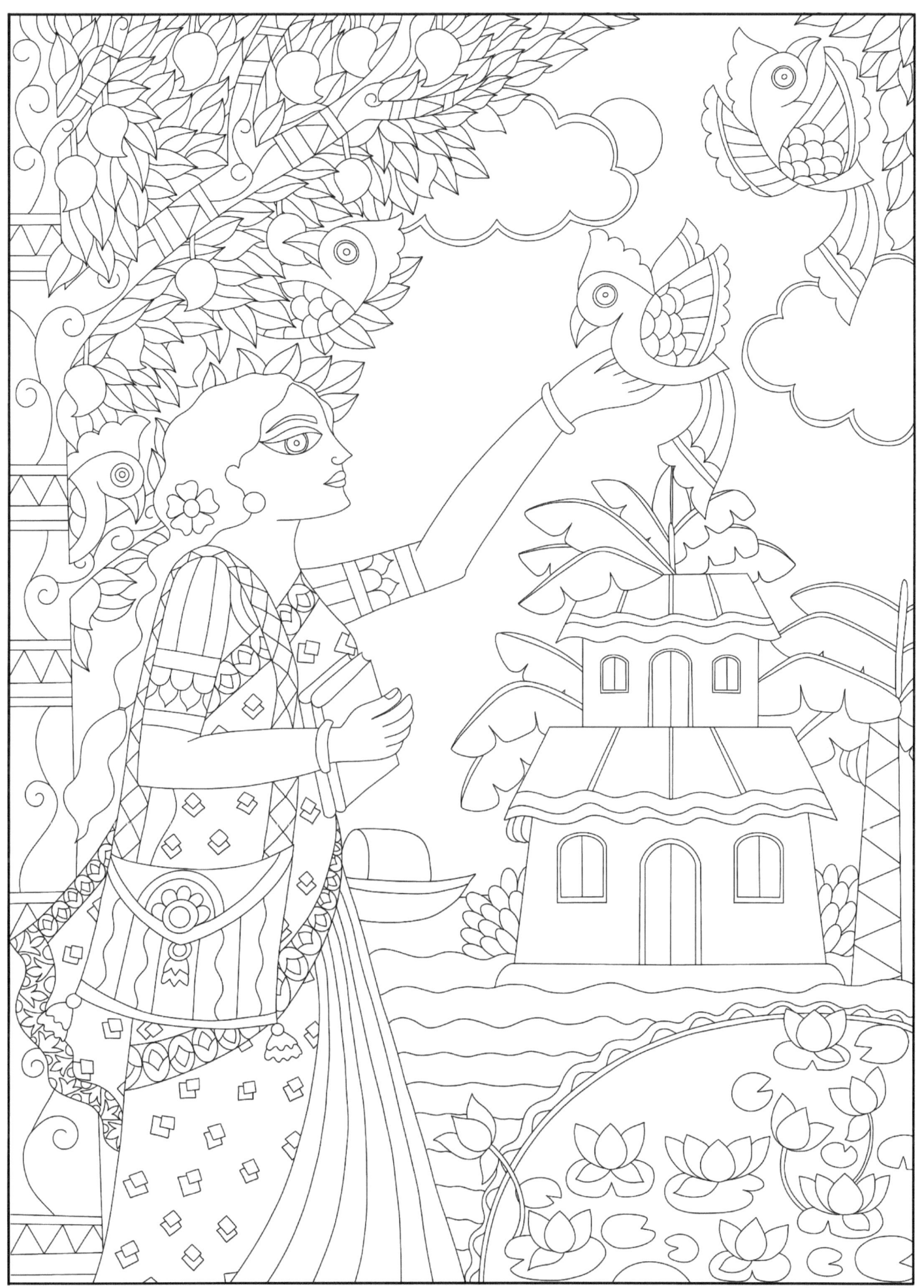

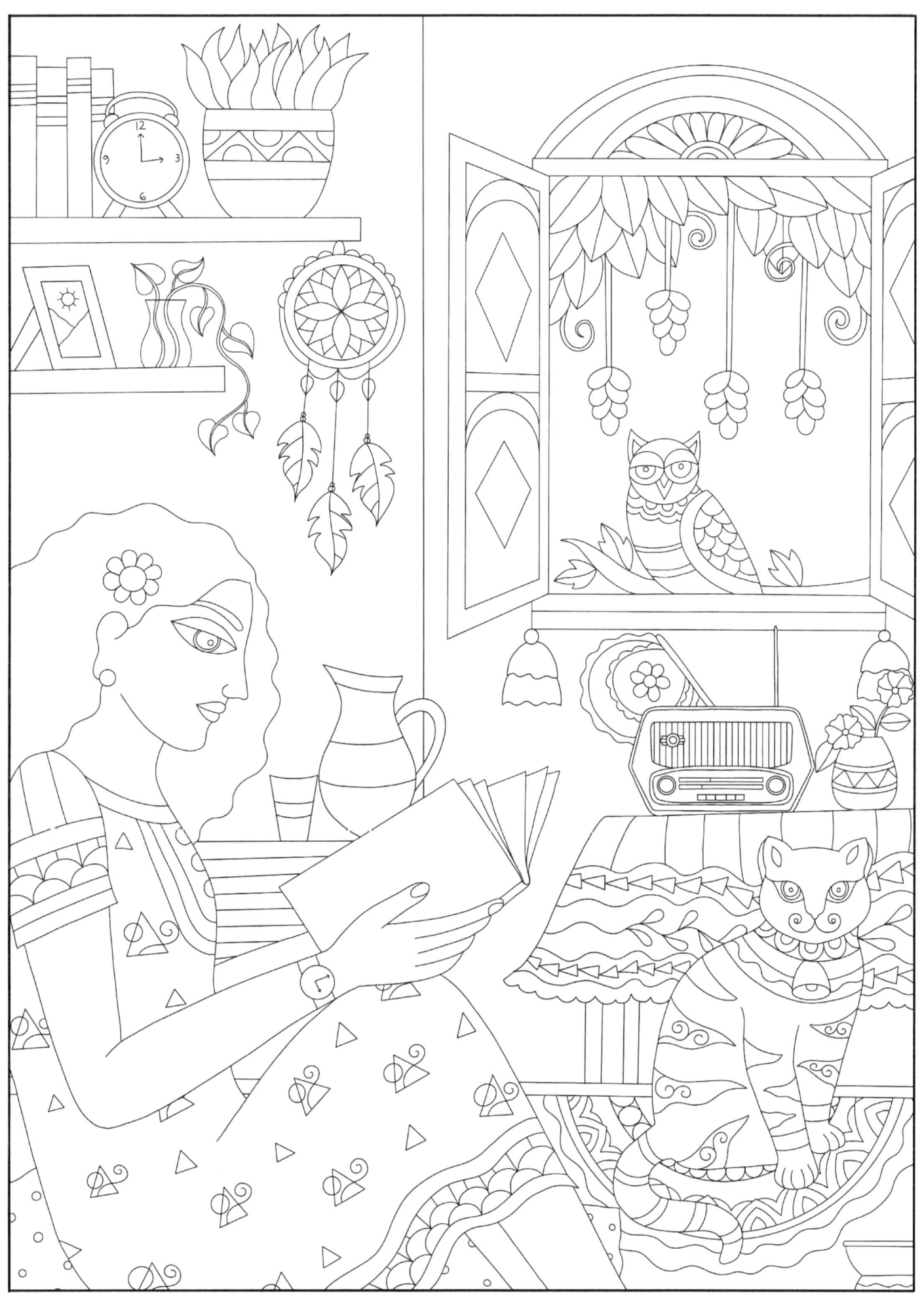

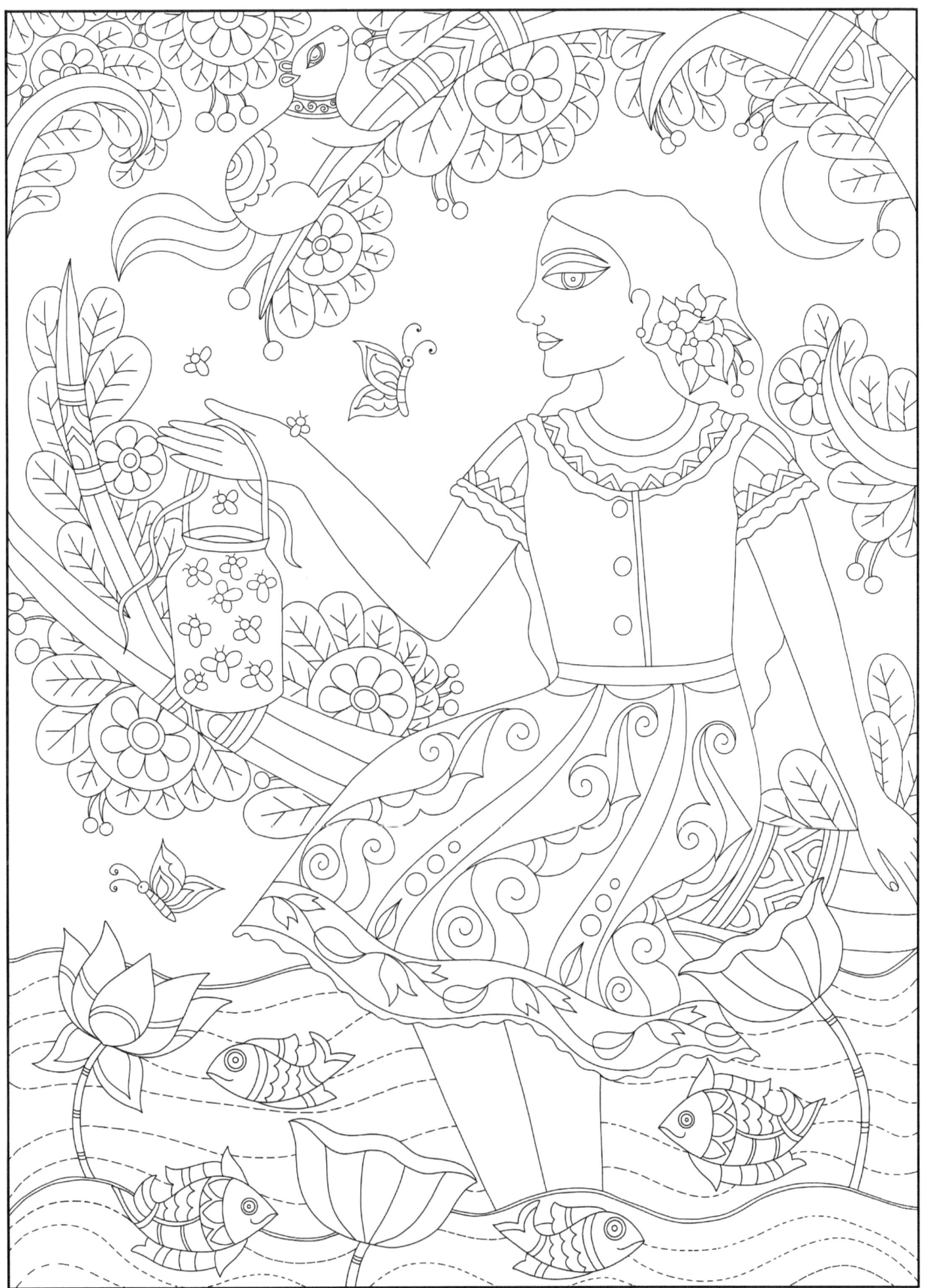

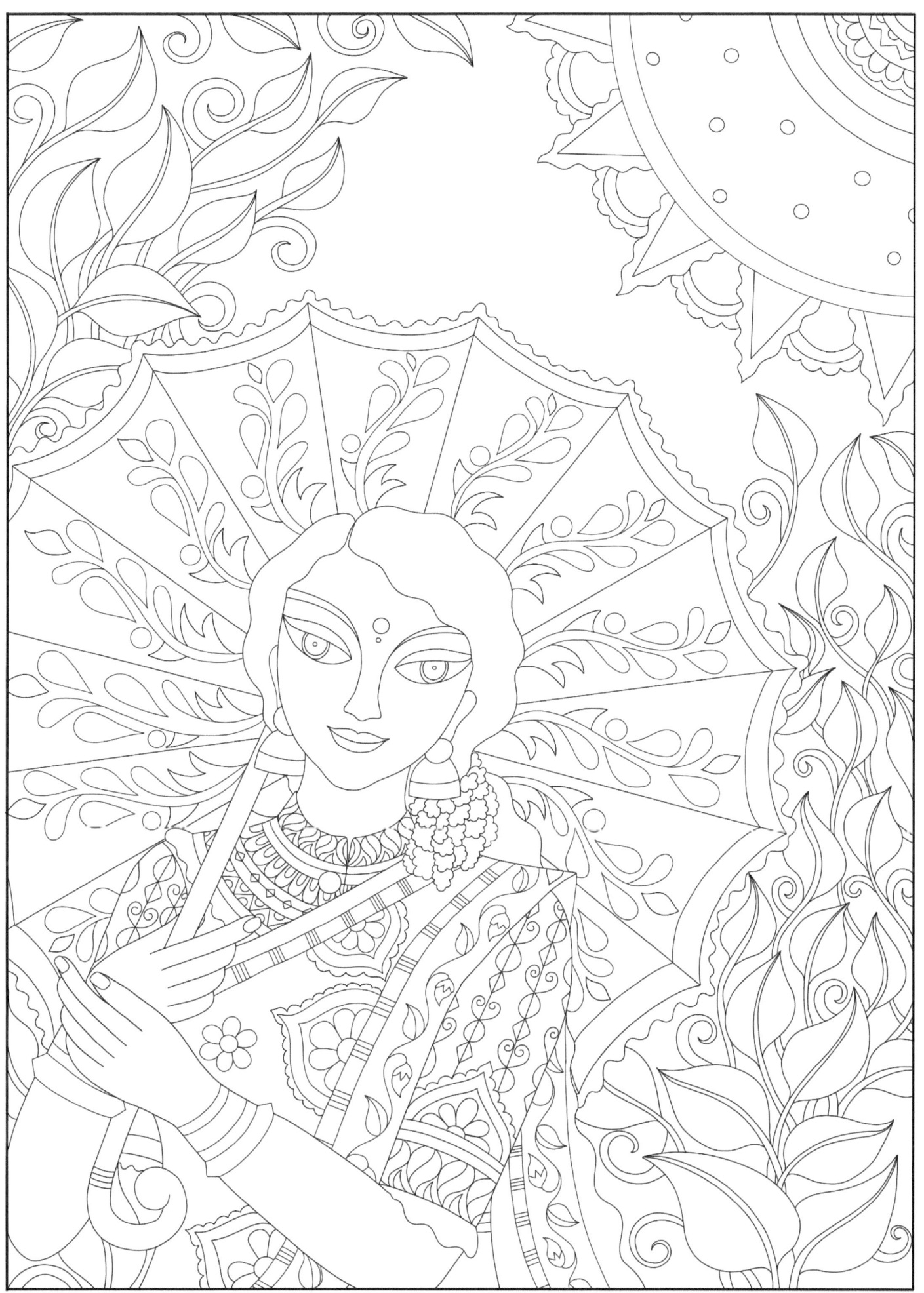

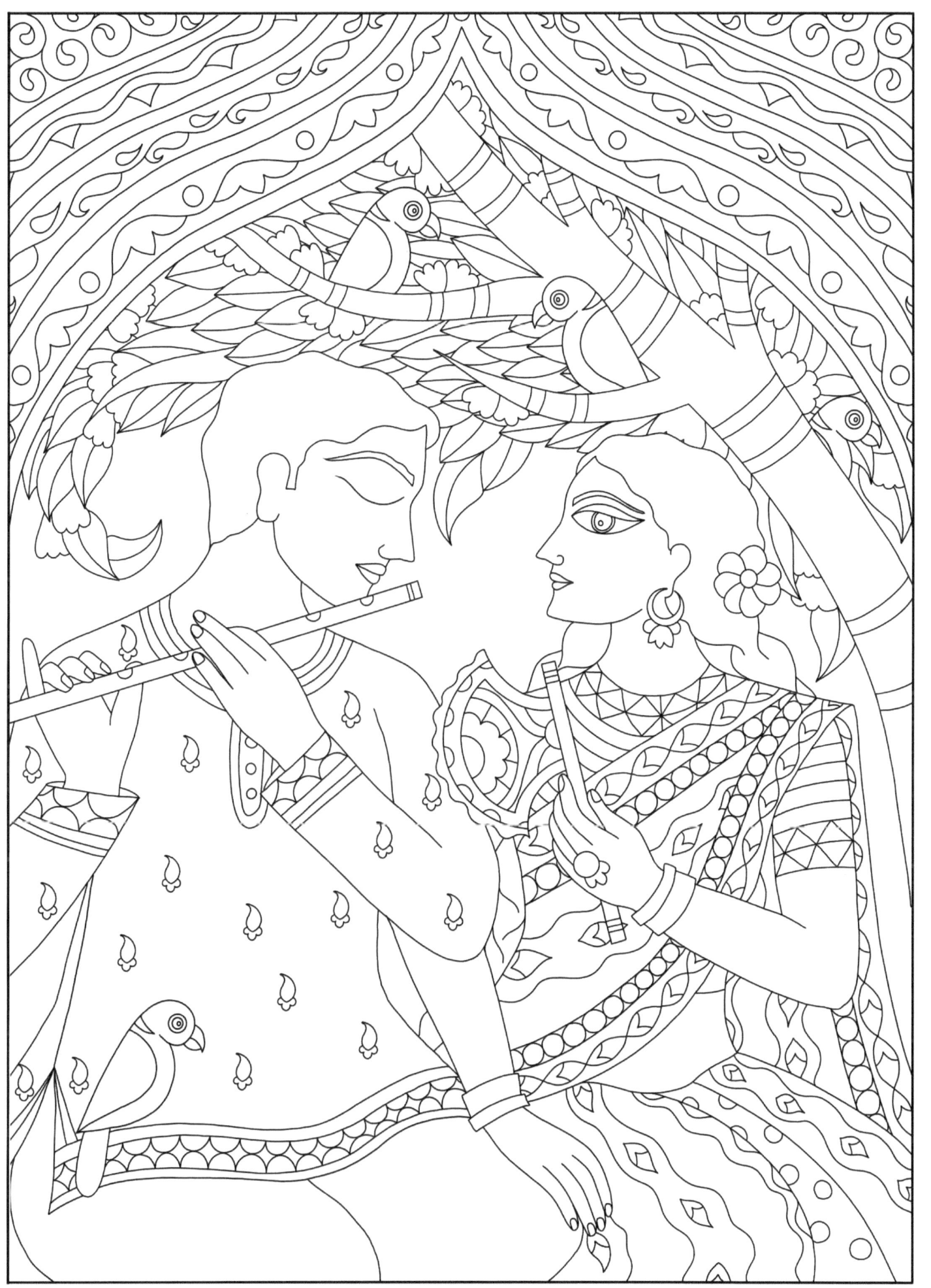

www.ingramcontent.com/pod-product-compliance
Lightning Source LLC
Chambersburg PA
CBHW040455220526
45473CB00004B/1640